Dr. Deborah D

Pray Through It

outskirts
press

Contents

About the Author

Dr. Deborah D. Dancy resides in Boston, Massachusetts with her 2 sons Colby Dancy-Chandler & Dana Dancy-Chandler. She has 2 grandchildren Talitha & Colby Jr. She is the proud daughter of Boston Public School teachers: James & Anna Mae Dancy. She is the elder daughter of 7 siblings.

Dr. Dancy is a well known preacher, educator, author and activist in pursuit of justice, equity and excellence. Throughout her career, she has touched the lives of thousands of young people, staff members and parents throughout the Commonwealth of Massachusetts.

Dr. Dancy is a Daughter of Zion. She has faithfully served the Lord for decades as laity, missionary, choir member, Christian educator, steward, trustee and preacher. She follows in the footsteps of her late uncle, John Campbell Dancy, Editor of the Star of Zion and Professor at Livingstone College.

Dr. Dancy is recognized nationally and internationally for her numerous contributions to the field of education. Amongst her many state-wide accolades, she has served as President of the Massachusetts Principal's Association and the Black Educators' Alliance of Massachusetts. Appointed from the United States Senate, out of Washington D.C., she holds the international distinction as a Fulbright Scholar. She is listed in Who's Who Amongst Female Executives and Who's Who In America. She is the author of 3 books: "Yes We Can! Strategies To Close The Achievement Gap"; "Count Me In! Inclusion Strategies for All" and "Pray Through It" which was released Spring 2019. All are available through major book stores. She is a proud life-time member of Delta Sigma Theta Sorority and recipient of the Livingstone College Leadership Award. She has achieved many accomplishments as a pioneer and advocate for the rights of women and people of color.

Dr. Dancy is a life-long learner. She is a Doctoral Graduate in Educational Leadership from Nova Southeastern University@ Ashwood with a Masters Degree from UMass Boston. She earned her Bachelor's Degree from Lesley College in Education and Clinical Psychology. In addition, she has completed post-graduate studies at Harvard University, Suffolk Law School, Northeastern University, International Bible Teaching School and Boston University.

In 2013, Dr. Dancy retired from the Boston Public Schools with 37 years of exemplary service. Currently, she is a full time Minister/ Student of the Gospel and strives to stay in God's Will. She is a God Chaser !!!

Suggested Prayers and Bible Passages

I encourage you to read and study these popular prayers and biblical passages for they have stood the test of time.

I will Lift Up Mine Eyes Unto The Hills
Prayer of Saint Assisi
Serenity Prayer
The Lord is My Shepherd
The Lord's Prayer

1 Corinthians 16:13
Ecclesiastes 3
Ephesians 6
James 5:15
John 3:16-17
Psalm 84:1
Psalm 96:10
Psalm 107:20
Psalm 139:2-3
Romans 12:2
Song of Solomon 1:1-2
Song of Solomon 1:7

Preface

While prayer should come natural, it is one of the hardest tasks to begin. It should be natural to commune with our Heavenly Father. It should be in our nature to connect with our Creator. But, the world has created a disconnect which makes this blessing so difficult to grasp.

I fervently believe that the prayers of the righteous are heard. I strongly believe that when JESUS died on the cross, for all of our sins, that we all received His Grace of forgiveness. I wholeheartedly believe that JESUS loves us unconditionally. I unequivocally believe that prayer is a necessity. We were born to praise the Lord. He deserves all of the glory and all of our honor.

Prayer is a neccessity. It is our opportunity to talk directly to our Heavenly Father without an intercessor. Unlike the days of the Old Testament, we do not require a spokesperson, a mediator or a translator. GOD understands us as we speak in our many diverse languages from all around the world. GOD understands us even if we're literate or illiterate. GOD communes with us through our tears of pain and tears of joy. We must pray in and out of season. We must pray whether we're happy, sad or somewhere in-between.

Prayer is food to our souls. It is our daily bread and water. It gives us hope. It gives us insight. It gives us peace. It gives us prosperity. It gives us love. It gives us joy. It gives us wisdom. Whatever we need or seek to know should be taken to GOD first in prayer. GOD is our ultimate counselor, mentor, lawyer, doctor, lover and friend. GOD will supply all of our health, wisdom, relationship, financial and other needs according to His Word.

While a prayer life is difficult to start, we must communicate with GOD. Prayer is a life time process which deepens as our faith and deeds increase. Our faith seed over time will produce results from our prayer life of supernatural impact. While not all inclusive or sequential, I have found this process/ means of praying to be helpful as I talk to my Heavely Father.

1. Read manuscripted prayers silently from the The Holy Bible and other sources. I recommend the Book of Psalms from the The Holy Bible as I consider The Holy Bible to be "the book of life". If you read no other book, I encourage you to read this one. It is your guide book, inspired by your Creator, on how to live your life. Everything has a system from which it operates-cars, computers, airplanes, microwaves and all of creation. A fish does not demonstrate its beauty and agility when taken out of water. As a matter of fact it eventually dies. So it is with (wo)man when we do not operate under the guidance of CHRIST and His system. We do not fulfill our unique destiny as purposed by our Creator.

2. Read manuscripted prayers out loud. There is power in the tongue. Speak into existence what you want and what you need. Our Heavenly Father wants to give us all of the blessings outlined in The Holy Bible. We access these blessings by asking through faithful prayer while filled with a heart of gratitude.

3. Write manuscripted prayers from the bible and other sources that relate to what you want to say to GOD. Through visual, auditory,

touch, movement, taste and smell you begin to internalize these messages as you write them down. The universe is your guide.

4. Pray what is on your heart silently throughout the day. Be still and listen for the presence of the Holy Spirit. It may be a simple prayer. It may be three or four words. It may be as simple as "Guide me LORD"... "Thank you Father"...GOD wants to be recognized in everything that we say, do or think.

5. Pray what is on your heart out loud throughout the day. Everday as you open your eyes, speak to The LORD "Thank you LORD for allowing me to see another day in this land of the living". Talk to Him about what you need for the day. Thank him for what He has done, is currently doing and is going to do for you in the future. There is power in the tongue. Give Him praise !!!

6. Pray for others silently and outloud. We are our brothers keeper. We are all connected as a part of the human race with one Father. Release your prayers of encouragement and love into the universe. The karma that you send out will be returned to you. I encourage you to send out love, joy, peace and prosperity.

7. Join prayer groups through your local church, prayer lines, organizations or social media. Pray with a strong bible-based group of believers. They will guide and support you in your prayer life. There are many to choose from within the Christian Faith.

8. Utilize a daily Christian electronic and/or written devotional prayer service. They will email/text you daily prayers free of charge on a variety of topics. Go to their websites to locate manuscripted prayers or to request mailed copies. Also, your local church can provide you with seasonal or specific prayers related to the church calendar ie Advent, Epiphany, Easter. Adapt words to meet your needs.

9. Pray at scheduled and unscheduled times throughout the day. Most

of us pray when we wake up, over meals and at bed-time. There are no limitations as to when you can speak to GOD. You may be on the job, driving your car, under the hair dryer or shopping at the supermarket. Just take a moment to thank GOD for the blessings He bestowed upon you. The fact that we can see the sky, hold a baby, feel the sunshine, touch the grass, kiss a loved one, walk in the rain and smell the roses is a blessing. GOD's world is beautiful. He supplies all of our needs according to His Word.

10. Make your prayer life a priority. Do not allow distractions to keep you from praying as this is the work of the enemy. Our GOD is a jealous GOD. And rightfully so, as He created us in His image above all that He created. He wants to be first in our life. He wants us to recognize Him first. He wants us to give to Him first. He wants us to talk to Him first. He wants us to listen to Him first. In all that we do, we must get His understanding.

11. Set aside an area for your scheduled prayer. It can be a prayer closet, your deck, bedroom, bathroom, car or church altar. Anywhere that you will be everyday at a regularly scheduled/uninterrupted time. While I pray throughout the day, I find it very helpful to pray/meditate first thing in the morning and before I close my eyes at night. This is my private time to welcome in and close out my day with my Creator to guide me. It is important to remember that not only do you want to talk to GOD; but, you want to listen for GOD's response. Pray with expectations and know that He hears you.

12. Journal your prayers to monitor your needs, focus and progress. You will be amazed at how many prayers GOD has answered for you. There are prayer journals on-line or you can simply use a notebook. I would encourage you not to complicate this wonderful blessing.

13. Lead others in corporate prayer at home, family gatherings, church or community services. Our nation is hurting. Our people are hurting.

We need prayer. GOD is the only one that can remove or lighten the burdens. The people you are praying for may not know this. But, if GOD has called you to lead them in prayer, you know. Now, you must take leadership in helping them to develop their prayer life. I know personally, that prayer moves mountains. I know personally, that prayer turns tests into testimonies. I know that, I have a personal relationship with GOD that is made sweeter through prayer.

14. Start a prayer group in your home, church or digital medium. You can utilize social media, teleconferences, video conferences and other technological means. Hold breakfast, luncheon or dinner sessions where you lift The LORD in prayer. People like to fellowship. Find ways to bring GOD's people together. Remember, we are all GOD's people. However, some don't know it and others haven't studied the operational manual (GOD's Word-The Holy Bible").

15. Get in a good Christian bible based/praying church where the Pastor and Congregation actively listen to and act on the Word of GOD. I can not stress this enough. We were created to praise the Lord, to fellowship and to reproduce/multiply. Don't try to do everything by yourself. Reach out and ask for help. In your reaching out, you may help inspire or save some other soul. This world is filled with trials and tribulations. But, we must stand firm in the knowledge that, there is power in the Word of GOD. We can never pray to much. So let us begin...."Our Father who art in heaven hallowed be thy name..."

Prayers of Faith

The Lord's Prayer

Our Father who art in heaven

Hallowed be thy name

Thy kingdom come

Thy will be done

On earth as it is in heaven

Give us this day our daily bread

And forgive us our trespasses

As we forgive those who trespass against us

Lead us not into temptation

But deliver us from evil

For thine is the kingdom, the power and the glory

Forever and Ever

Amen

The Lord Is My Shepherd
Psalm 23

The LORD is my shepherd I shall not want.

He maketh me to lie down in green pastures.

He leadeth me beside the still waters.

He restoreth my soul.

He leadeth me in the paths of righteousness for His name's sake.

Yea though I walk through the valley of the shadow of death I will fear no evil for thou art with me.

Thy rod and thy staff they comfort me.

Thou prepares a table before me in the presence of mine enemies.

Thou anointest my head with oil.

My cup runneth over.

Surely goodness and mercy shall follow me all the days of my life.

And I will dwell in the house of the LORD forever.

Amen

Lamb of Calvary
James 5:15

My faith looks up to thee... Oh Lamb of Calvary...Saviour Divine... Please hear me while I pray...Take all my sins away...Oh let me from this day be ever thine.

Your word tells us "And the prayer of faith shall save the sick, and the LORD shall raise him up; and if he have committed sins, they shall be forgiven him".

I will pray in and out of seasons. I will anoint my head with oil. I will seek out my elders. I will dwell in the House of the LORD forever. By my faith, I am healed and free from sin.

Amen

A Mountain Top Experience

Oh Lord GOD you are mighty and everlasting.

You are beyond our knowing.

Yet we see your glory in the righteousness of Christ whose compassion illuminates and transfigures the world.

We pray that you would transform/change us into the likeness of Christ who received our humanity so that we might share in His divinity.

Reveal the glory and presence of your Spirit alive in the world today, free us from all doubts and empower us to act as transfigured/changed people.

Change us Oh GOD and make us more like you. Grant us Oh GOD a mountain top experience.

Amen

I Can't Go Back

Lord help me to keep moving forward. I need faith to not look back. I can not look back because there is nothing that I want to go back to in this season of my life. My looking back means nothing but pain, despair, anger, rejection and loss.

I need you to work a miracle in my life Lord for somewhere I read.... somewhere I heard.... that you are a miracle worker. I am all the way in your pool of mercy. I will not flirt with you. I will not betray you. I will not turn my face from you.

I need you Lord in a very special way. I need your Shekinah Glory. This is my hour. This is my time. This is my season to enlarge my territory. I do not believe you brought me this far to leave me.

My faith looks up to thee Oh Lamb of Calvary....Saviour Divine.... Order my steps Dear Lord and I will acknowledge you in all my ways.

Amen

Commit

Oh Lord GOD how excellent is thy name above all the earth, sky, heavens and sea. My faith in you causes me to commit my entire being to you. Everything that I am or hope to be I owe to you.

I will commit my ways to you in the good and bad times. I will trust only in you for you are the same GOD yesterday, today and tomorrow. I will trust and believe in you for you have never failed me yet.

I commit myself to you Lord to be a living sacrifice pleasing in your sight. I pray that you will increase my faith, guide my footsteps, control my tongue and use me in your Kingdom.

Amen

Triumph

Oh Lord my faith cries out that I will triumph in the works ordered by your hands. You have created this masterpiece to be a part of the Body of Christ. Make plain the destiny you have designed for me Oh Lord.

Anoint me with fresh oil Oh Lord so that I may stand against my enemies, principalities and spirits of darkness. Strengthen my mind and body with your righteousness.

Help me to bring forth good fruit so that all under the sound of my voice may feast and flourish. My faith claims the riches of this land as provided by your bountiful blessings.

Amen

One Body

Oh Lord Our Heavenly Father...We thank you for the Body of Christ. We thank you for your boundless love.

You have commanded us to operate in unity. So help the eye to work with the mouth; the mouth to work with the ear; the ear to work with the hand and the hand to work with the foot. For, we are all one in Your Kingdom. No one part is greater than the entire body.

Help us to understand that, as a part of your body, we were created to shine like the bright and morning star. Help us to understand that, as a part of your body, we were created to carry out your works.

Release the wisdom that you have placed inside of us. Give us faith the size of a mustard seed. Order our steps Dear Lord. We give you all of the praise and all of the glory In Jesus Name.

Amen

The Battle

Father I stretch my hands to you for no other help I know. Help me to overcome jealousy, misery, envy and strife.

Give me the faith that helps me to forgive; to show compassion; to create and to give my best to you as master.

Restore unto me my joy and my salvation. Restore unto me the peace, like a river, that can come only from you Lord.

Strengthen my faith. Gird my loins. Prepare my hands for battle for I am a soldier in your army Oh God.

Amen

Seasons
Ecclesiastes 3

Heavenly Father I know that whatever you do will last forever; nothing can be added to it; and nothing can be taken away. I revel and kneel in awe of your omnipotent power for I know that...

To everything there is a season and a time to every purpose under the heaven.

A time to be born and a time to die; a time to plant, and a time to pluck up that which is planted.

A time to kill, and a time to heal; a time to break down and a time to build up.

A time to cast away stones and a time to gather stones together; a time to embrace and a time to refrain from embracing.

A time to get and a time to lose; a time to keep and a time to cast away.

A time to tear and a time to mend; a time to keep silent and a time to speak.

A time to love and a time to hate; a time of war and a time of peace.

My faith Oh GOD rests in you for you have made everything beautiful in your time. Help me to hold out until my change of season has come.

Amen

Prayers of Hope

I Will Lift Up Mine Eyes
Psalm 121

Father...I will lift up mine eyes unto the hills from whence cometh my help.

My help cometh from the Lord which made heaven and earth.

He will not suffer my foot to be moved; He that keepeth me will not slumber.

Behold He that keepeth Israel shall neither slumber nor sleep.

The Lord is my keeper.

The Lord is my shade upon my right hand.

The sun shall not smite me by day, nor the moon by night.

The Lord shall preserve me from all evil; He shall preserve my soul.

The Lord shall preserve my going out and coming in from this time forth and even for evermore.

Amen

Prayer for Healing
Psalm 107:20

Dear GOD-Your Word in Psalm 107:20 says that you send out your Word and heal.

I stand on your Word and I pray that you would send your healing Word to me right now.

I petition you to drive all sickness and infirmity from my body.

I request that you strengthen my family and loved ones during my time of need.

I ask that through this time of trials and tribulation may your name continue to be glorified.

All of this I pray in the magnificient Name of JESUS !

Amen

Salvation

My LORD what a morning when the sun refuses to shine.

My mind is confused

My body aches

My spirit is weak

My voice is silent

My LORD, I need you today in a very special way.

Give me clarity

Give me strength

Give me peace

Give me your words

My LORD restore unto me thy salvation and I will continue to walk in your ways and praise your Holy Name.

Amen

Eternal Father

GOD of our weary years

GOD of our silent tears

Thou who has brought us thus far

On our way....

We thank you for waking us up this morning

We thank you for another day's journey in the land of the living

We thank you for your world and all of its beauty

We honor you Eternal Father

We glorify your Holy Name

We praise you Lord

Keep us forever in your path we pray

Amen

Sweet Hour of Prayer

Oh Lord My GOD I adore you and I magnify your Holy Name.

I thank you for this sweet hour of prayer that calls me from a world of care and places me at your throne.

I thank you for this sweet hour of prayer where I can talk to you and make all of my wishes and wants known.

I know that in all of my seasons of distress and grief my soul will find relief.

I know that I will escape the tempter's snare as long as I can commune with you in a sweet hour of prayer.

Amen

Supernatural Help

Father GOD I no longer want to be anxious about this problem. I ask for your supernatural help.

I want to rest in your grace and mercy. I ask for your supernatural help.

I turn over this burden to you. I ask for your supernatural help.

I know that it is in your hands. I ask for your supernatural help.

I know that you are in charge. I ask for your supernatural help.

I know that all is well. I ask for your supernatural help.

Saviour Divine, I thank you for relieving me of this burden through your supernatural help.

Amen

In Times of Distress

In times of distress I will call upon you Lord for I know you will answer me. When deep in my soul I feel empty you are always there.

In times of distress I will look for the God in me. I will look to the God that resides in this temple for your Holy Spirit speaks to me.

In times of distress I will not fear the valley or the mountaintop for you are with me. While in the valley, I know you will bring me up out of the pits of hell. Likewise, when on the mountaintop, I know you will cover me and catch me should I stumble or fall.

In times of distress, I will not turn away from you. I will give you shouts of grateful praise for I know my Salvation comes from you. You are My Lord....My GOD.....My Everything.

Amen

Beauty For Ashes

Oh Lord GOD how excellent is thy name !

I do not know what tomorrow will bring. I do not know why my loved one was taken by the death angel. I do not know why I can't get a job that I thought I was a perfect fit. But, I know you will give me beauty for my ashes.

I do not know why my children are not living up to their calling. I do not know why there is so much pain. I do not know why there is such a strong feeling of rejection. But, I know you will give me beauty for ashes.

I do not know why my body is riddled with pain. I do not know why I suffer from drug addiction, arthritis, cancer, alzheimer or diabetes. I do not know why your children suffer from oppression, recession and depression.

But, I do know this, if we just keep hope alive, you will give us beauty for our ashes.

Amen

Come Ye Disconsolate

Oh Father GOD I am filled with adoration for you are the hope of the disconsolate; the joy of the desolate and the Bread of Life.

I bring my wounded heart and fervently kneel before the mercy seat for I know that earth has no sorrow that heaven can not heal.

I bring my emptiness and seek overflow from the Holy Comforter for I know that earth has no sorrow that heaven can not cure.

I come before you Lord seeking the Living Water pure from above. I come before you seeking the Feast of Love for earth has no sorrow that heaven is not able to remove.

You are my hope, my strength and my redeemer. It is in JESUS Name I pray.

Amen

O Thou in Whose Presence
Song of Solomon 1:7

O Thou in whose presence my soul take delight

On whom in all affliction I will call

You are my comforter by day

You are my song in the night

You are my hope and my salvation

You are my ALL !!!

Amen

Prayers of Love

I Want to Be Where You Are

Oh Mighty GOD...Lord of the universe...I want to be where you are...

Whatever you are making or breaking

Don't do it without me.

Whatever you are bending or mending

Don't do it without me.

Whatever you are fixing or mixing

Don't do it without me.

Forever keep me in your presence where true love abounds. In the Name of Jesus I pray.

Amen

Your Love

My Lord your fragrance is sweeter than the scent of my best perfume.

Your touch is more gentle than the wings of a beloved dove.

Your face is more beautiful than the colorful lilies of the field.

Your love for me bears witness in the beauty of the rose.

Your love for me bears witness in the splendor of the rainbow.

May my love for you bear witness in everything that I think, say and do.

Amen

I Will Follow

Wherever you are Lord

Embrace me in your mighty arms

Keep me in the palm of your hands

I will follow because I want to be where you are my friend.

Wherever you are Lord

Leave your powerful, loving footprints

Make the pathway plain for my spirit to see

I will follow because I just want to be where you are; for you are my rock, my redeemer and my everlasting love.

Amen

Prayer of Assissi

Lord, make me an instrument of thy peace. Where there is hatred, let me sow love.

Lord, grant that I might not so much seek to be loved as to love.

Where there is injury, pardon.

Where there is doubt, faith.

Where there is despair, hope.

Where there is darkness, light.

Where there is sadness, joy.

O Divine Master, grant that I may not so much seek to be consoled as to console...To be understood as to understand...To be loved as to love.

For it is in giving that we receive. It is in pardoning that we are pardoned. It is in dying to self that we are born to eternal life.

Amen

Eternal Life

John 3:16-17

For GOD so loved the world that he gave his one and only Son, that whosoever believes in him shall not perish but have eternal life.

For GOD did not send his Son into the world to condemn the world, but to save the world though him.

I fall prostrate before you in prayer for eternal life.

Teach me your ways LORD and keep me in your will for you are GOD alone.

Amen

Unspeakable Joy

Oh LORD, I have Joy, Joy, Joy deep in my soul. This Joy I have, the world didn't give it to me and the world can't take it away.

Even though, I am always going to, in the midst of or coming out of a storm; I still have my joy.

I just want to take time out of my busy day to thank you for your umbrella of love, grace and mercy.

LORD, I thank you for this unspeakable joy and I will continue to give you all of the praise, the glory and the honor.

Amen

Unconditional Love

Dear LORD....

I am so happy

Resting in your arms

I love you LORD

Amen

Love in the Dark Places

Oh Heavenly Father you have revealed the glory of your love for me through Jesus Christ and by giving me your Holy Spirit.

Help me to listen to the Holy Spirit and to faithfully follow the Words of Jesus Christ. Guide me in the dark places, where you send me and help me to reveal the light of your Gospel of Love.

Amen

Resting in His Love

LORD we thank you for this time when we can just enter into your rest.

LORD we thank you for loving us.

LORD we thank you for the peace that passes all understanding.

In the Name of JESUS.

Amen

The Garden

I come to the garden alone while the dew is still on the roses. Oh LORD I see you in the Garden of Gethsemane. I hear you as you ask your disciples to watch with you. I feel your pain as man turns against you.

Your people are in pain LORD as we struggle with bills, health, relationships, incarceration, employment and we give you thanks. We give you our love for your ways are not fickle like those of man.

We love you for watching over us for we are nothing without you. We thank you for walking with us and talking with us and telling us that we are your own. The joy that we share as we meet in your garden; no other has ever known.

LORD we love you...

LORD we adore you...

LORD we praise your holy name for you are worthy to be praised!

Amen

Knowledge of God
Psalm 139:2-3

Oh Lord GOD I delight in my knowledege of you. For to know you is to love you. And to love you is to want to obey you.

I walk in your love and charity. You know my sitting down and my rising up. You know all of my ways and yet you love me.

I thank you Lord for loving me. When I go astray, I pray that you will bring me back to your path of love and charity .

Amen

Equally Yoked

Help me Father GOD to be equally yoked with a mate that knows and understands for....

My love is deeper than the ocean

My love flows like a mighty stream

My love shines like a diamond

Help me Father GOD to be equally yoked with a mate that knows and understands for....

My love is not a one act kind-of-love

My love is not a one room kind-of-love

My love is not a one night kind-of-love

Help me Father GOD to be equally yoked with a mate that knows and follows you for....

Your love is bright like the morning star

Your love is eternal

Your love brings peace to my soul

Amen

Kiss Me with Your Lips

Solomon 1:1-2

Kiss me over and over again with your mouth for your lips are sweeter than wine.

When you kiss me with your mouth I am free from pain... guilt... fear.

When you kiss me with your lips I feel joy....I feel peace....I feel love.

Kiss me over and over again with your mouth for your lips are sweeter than wine.

Thank you LORD for loving me unconditionally.

Amen

Prayers of Courage

Serenity Prayer

GOD, grant me the the serenity

to accept the things

I can not change.

The courage to change the things I can.

And, the wisdom to know the difference.

Amen

God Reigns Forever

What a marvelous GOD we serve.

You are the same GOD yesterday, today and tomorrow.

We come today LORD to proclaim your birth, death and resurrection.

We are blessed to eat from your bread of life and to drink from the cup that symbolizes your blood.

Help us to wait for your return.

Help us to desire your heart.

Help us to watch for you.

Help us to to be ready when you come.

LORD bless us with courage so that we may live and reign with The Father, The Son and The Holy Spirit now and throughout eternity.

Amen

Stand Fast
1 Corinthians 16:13

Oh GOD of the Universe...I seek your face during

good times and times of trials and

tribulation...Whatever my season may be, you are

my rock and my shield...Help me to watch, stand

fast in the faith and to be strong. You are my

provider, my healer and my deliverer. I can fight

any battle for I get my courage from you.

Amen

Fountain of Life

Oh Lord My GOD...

How excellent is thy name.

You rule the earth, the sky and the waters.

My faith flows from you.

My hope flows from you.

My charity flows from you.

My joy flows from you.

My prosperity flows from you.

My peace flows from you.

My courage flows from you.

You are my Fountain of Life and I love you.

Amen

Courage for These Times
Ephesians 6

Oh Lord My GOD....I pray for fortitude-for courage

I will put on your full armour Oh Lord.

I will gird my loins with truth.

I will put on the breastplate of righteousness.

I will shod my feet with the gospel of peace.

I will take the helmet of salvation.

I will fight with the sword of the Spirit which is your word Oh GOD.

And above all I will win this battle with my shield of faith.

No dark forces will stop me from the fullness of my destiny.

I will continuously pray in supplication to the Holy Spirit for fortitude-for courage.

I am a soldier in the Army of The Lord.

I will fight for GOD's Kingdom to reign forever.

Use me Oh Lord in your power and your might.

Amen

Resting in the Almighty

Thank you LORD that in the midst of my trials and tribulations you are teaching me to rest in You The Almighty.

Thank you LORD for giving me the confidence in knowing that you are stronger than any forces that threaten me.

Thank you LORD for being my protector and provider through seen and unseen dangers, toils and snares.

Resting in you, I find a peace that passes all understanding. It is in the matchless name of Jesus that I pray.

Amen

How Lovely Are Thy Dwellings
Psalm 84:1

How lovely are thy dwellings Oh Lord of Hosts.

My soul longs for and seeks out the courts of the Lord.

My heart and my flesh cry out for You the Living GOD.

I would rather spend a day in your courts than a thousand in the world.

Bless me Lord, with the Gifts of The Holy Spirit, for I stand on your promises.

Bless my inward and outward dwellings so that all will see the fruit of your mighty hand.

I will continue to walk in your authority in the name of JESUS.

Amen

No Good Thing

LORD I walk in your favor.

I walk in your grace.

I walk in your promise that no good thing will be witheld from those who walk in your righteousness.

You are the one and only GOD and I honor you.

Hear my humble prayer Oh LORD.

Amen

Demons

Oh My LORD, please remove all impure thoughts from my worldly mind.

Cleanse me of all addictions.

Heal my body of affliction.

Remove all demonic forces from my home.

Give me a clean heart and a discerning spirit so that I may serve you.

In The Name Of JESUS...

Amen

Strength

I now enter my inner sanctuary and speak to the GOD that resides in me for I know...

I am the righteousness of GOD.

I am holy in GOD.

I am sanctified in GOD.

I am delivered in GOD.

I can do all things in My GOD who strengthens me.

Speak to me Holy Spirit for you are welcome in this place.

Amen

Prayers of Justice

The Final Judge

Almighty and Eternal GOD, I pray for justice and equity today. There is so much pain, anger, poverty, violence and treachery in our world today.

Help me to be my brother's keeper.

Strengthen my body for the long journey. Use my hands for social and political justice.

Give me wisdom and discernment in your ways of justice and equity.

You are the final judge over the righteous and the wicked for there is a time for every matter and every work.

There is a season for everything.

You are the beginning and the end.

You are the Alpha and the Omega.

Oh LORD, on that final day of judgement, I want to be found in your will. In the Name of JESUS...

Amen

You Will Fight My Battles

Oh Lord GOD....I am in trouble.

I am hanging on by a thread.

I believe there is no turbulent storm that you can not calm.

I believe there is no raging fire that you can not quench.

I believe that the battle is not mine; but, yours

Oh Lord.

Therefore, I am holding on because I know you are here and you will fight my battles.

Amen

Where Is the Justice

Oh Lord....Where is the justice?

Everday I watch the homeless walking the streets. No where to lay their heads, searching for food to eat, begging for money, trying to get a fix, looking for love in all the wrong places.

Oh Lord....When will it end?

Everday I watch what looks like the "walking dead" with faces filled with despair, pain and unrealized dreams.

Oh Lord....I know this is not your will.

As a member of the Body of Christ, please show me a way to be an instrument of peace, prosperity, love and justice.

Amen

Justice Is Blind

Oh Father....Our Lady of Liberty cries out for justice that is blind. Yet all around us the scales are weighted against your people based on color, race, economic status, gender, sexual preference and the list goes on.

Your Word tells us that you are the Father of us all. Yet, we are not treated equally. We are not treated justly.

Heavenly Father show me a way to be used as an instrument for peace, love, unity and most of all justice.

Amen

My Arms Are too Short

My arms are to short to box with you Oh GOD.

My ears had heard of you; but now, filled with love, my eyes see you.

My spirit feels the hot, passionate glow of your presence.

In justice and unity, I adorn myself with your glory and splendor.

As your child, I clothe myself with your honor and majesty.

Your reach spans the breadth of the oceans and the depths of the seas.

Your view stretches from the bowels of the earth to the heavens.

You know my inward, as well as, my outward thoughts.

Your word says that vengeance belongs only to you and he without sin should cast the first stone.

Help me to not judge my brothers and sisters for only you know their hearts.

Keep me from the den of the proud for you shall bring them low.

I pray for unity with you Lord because my arms are just to short to box with you Oh GOD !

Amen

No Justice

Heavenly Father help me to understand why there is no justice, no unity, no love amongst mankind.

Help me to understand why there is so much fighting, destruction, violence, discrimination...Tell me Father, "Why does the same crime get a different time?"

Your Word tells us that you created us in your own image and you are goodness, love and peace. So, tell me why there seems to be no justice; but "Just Us".

Amen

Choices

Oh Lord My GOD how excellent is thy name !

I praise you...I adore you...I worship you !! I lift your name on high !!!

Thank you for this wonderful day that you have blessed me with the opportunity to experience.

Thank you for giving me the option of choice...

The ability to choose how I will respond to this day.

Help me to make the right choices so that justice may be served. In your Holy Name I pray.

Amen

Rejoice
Psalm 96:10

Father I rejoice in you. I praise your Holy Name. Your Word tells me that your world is firmly established and cannot be moved. You will judge all mankind in fairness and equity.

As with all creation, I rejoice in you Oh Lord. Your Word tells me that upon your return, you will judge me by my righteousness and my faith.

Restore unto me a clean heart and renew a right spirit within me. I want to be ready to rejoice with you throughout eternity.

Amen

The Living Bread

Father GOD I Love you. I adore you. I praise your Holy Name.

My life is not always filled with peace and tranquility. There are many days of despair, turmoil and pain.

Through it all, I thank you for being the Living Bread that came down from heaven to die for my sins and transgressions.

In Holy Communion, I willingly partake of your bread as a representation of your flesh. I willingly drink the wine as the embodiment of your blood.

In doing so, my faith assures me that I will be raised up on the last day and that I will have eternal life in your Kindom of Glory.

But, while I am still down here on this earth with all of its evil and wicked ways; please don't forget about me Lord.

I will continue to praise you and lift Your Name on high.

Amen

Unity in Christ

Heavenly Father I lift your name on high. I adore you. I praise you. I magnify you in your glory.

I pray for unity in Christ. I am a part of the Body of Christ and I want to fulfill your mission over my life.

Guide me Great Jehovah. Equip me for the works of your service so that your Kingdom may be built up.

Help me obtain the full measure of the wholeness of GOD so that your people may prosper.

Connect me to the GOD in me where I may grow in love and unity so that your people will see you in me.

I thank you for all that you have done, are doing and will do in my life.

I will continue to lift your name in praise and to give you all of the glory and honor in Jesus name.

Amen

Prayers of Stewardship

The Gift

Heavenly Father, I thank you for the wonderful gift of life you have given me.

I thank you for the family and friends that you have provided for me.

I thank you for the gifts and talents you have given me.

Help me to always remember that all of these blessings come from you LORD.

I am nothing without you.

I glory in you as I make stewardship a part of my life.

I humbly accept and will continuously use this wonderful gift of life to praise and magnify your Holy Name.

Amen

Provisions

O Holy Spirit, I thank you for the provisions I need for they have already been made available.

Through my eyes of faith I see your manisfestations of

love

peace

joy

health

deliverance

And prosperity flowing abundantly in my life.

As your child, I rest in the confidence of you JESUS and what you have already done for me.

Amen

Enlarge My Territory

Oh Lord GOD I pray that you would bless me indeed. Rain down on me a blessing that I do not have room to receive. Bless me with your overflow. Father enlarge my territory and use me.

Keep your hand on me so that no evil shall come upon me. Give me a clean heart so that I may know the fullness of the God in me.

Cover me so that I may do good to the people and for the land. Creator of the Universe enlarge my territory and use me.

Amen

You Are My Shield

Oh My Lord how excellent is thy name. You are my shield when my enemies come against me.

There are those who do not believe in your power. But, I choose not to walk in their foolish ways.

I know you are a strong tower placing your shield of protection around me.

I lift my head high. I walk in your authority. I boldly call upon your name.

Each morning, I awaken to the joy of a new day. As evening falls, I rest upon your breast.

I rest peacefully in your arms for you are my shield.

Amen

The God in Me

Oh GOD be with me during the good and bad times.

Walk with me when I am in a storm; going into a storm or coming out of a storm for I know the rain falls on the just and the unjust.

Oh GOD increase the God in me so that I may feel your Holy Power. Help me to be one of your disciples who sees and works miracles in your name.

You are an awesome GOD and there is nothing to big or to grand for you. Give me the vision, provision and the courage to maximize the God in me.

Amen

Spirit of Poverty

In the Name of Jesus Christ of Nazareth I cast out the Spirit of Poverty. I will not be influenced by the Spirit of Mammon. Help me to receive in every area of my life. I stand firm under the covenant agreement over my life so that I may receive your promises of abundance.

Amen

Bless Me Father

Bless me Heavenly Father right now for at Your feet I humbly bow. Take my grief and pain away.

I call upon You this very hour to rain down upon me and fill me with Your magnificent grace and power.

Oh Lord it is your mercy that I plead during my troublesome hour of need.

You are the blessed one that shines like the radiant sun.

You are the brilliant light that shines within; even in the midst of my despair. Bless me now Father for I repent of my sin.

Amen

Storms

Oh Lord GOD I adore you and honor you for your grace and mercy.

I know that there is always a storm lingering near. I am either going into a storm, in a storm or coming out of a storm.

When there are struggles on my job, I pray for your protection.

When there are financial barriers and I have more month than money, I pray for your protection.

When there are struggles in my relationships with loved ones, I pray for your protection.

When I don't hear your voice or walk in your footsteps, I pray for your protection.

I thank you Lord for your protection; understanding that from every stormy wind that blows and every swelling tide of woes; there is a calm and sure retreat that is found beneath your mercy seat.

Amen

My Times Are in Your Hands

Oh Lord my times are in your hands. My GOD I am so glad that they are there. My life, my friends, my soul I leave entirely to your care.

Help me to be a good steward over the life and the provisions you have gifted me.

You have blessed me with life, health, strength, talents and skills to use and multiply during my daily walk, here on this earth. I pray for prudence, discipline and obedience to render fruit that meets with your approval.

Father my times are in your hands and I'll always trust in thee. When I am no longer in this earthly body, I pray that you will prepare an eternal resting place in heaven for me; because at your right hand is where I long to be.

Amen

Master of Space and Time

Heavenly Father You are the Master of Space and Time....

I seek not to understand all of the forces of your magnificient creation; but, to give thanks for being here amongst your earthly realm.

Light, water, air, earth and soul are all elements of my existence.

The idea of creation is beyond my human intellect and so I just accept you as the Great I Am ...

I offer up to you all of my gratitude for allowing me to be in the land of the living one more day.

Your Holy Spirit tells me that as it was in the beginning so shall it ever be, world without end for You are the Master of Space and Time.

Amen

Prayers of Temperance

Self-Control

Oh LORD, you are the model of temperance and self control.

I pray for the increase of moderation and self-restraint in my spirit.

My body is your temple.

It belongs only to you LORD.

I will not abuse it with sinful thoughts, alcohol, drugs, wrong or excessive foods.

Help me to keep my inward and outward body clean so that I may be a living sacrifice for you.

In the mighty Name of Jesus.

Amen

Healed by Your Stripes

I want to thank you Lord for my healing.

The devil thought he had me bound.

But, thank GOD through Your stripes I am healed.

Amen

Teach Me to Pray

Oh Lord teach me to pray

I humble myself before you

Oh Lord teach me to pray

I want to be a vessel for your kingdom

Oh Lord teach to me pray

Amen

In Your Presence

Lord GOD I come before you today wanting nothing but to be in your presence.

You are my joy, my peace, my strength like no other.

I love you beyond the stars. I adore you in all of your splendor.

I magnify your Holy Name.

Amen

My Walk

Oh My GOD help us to walk in your favor. We ask that you give us a clean heart so that we may serve you and glorify your Holy Name.

We ask that you keep our footsteps on the path of righteousness. We need you to help us walk your straight and narrow highway so that we may honor your Holy Name.

We ask that you bridle our tongues. We petition you to help us not say hurtful, deceitful words to ourselves or to our neighbors. We want to use our tongues to edify and praise your Holy Name.

Oh My GOD you alone deserve all of the glory, honor and praise. I will lift your name on high.

Amen

Use Me Lord

Speak Lord for your servant hears your voice.

My very being wants to serve you my Lord.

I was created to serve you

Use my eyes, my ears, my mouth, my hands, my arms, my legs, my feet to do your will.

I'll go where you tell me to go.

I'll say what you tell me to say.

I'll do what you tell me to do.

I am a part of the Body of Christ created in your image and filled with the Holy Spirit.

Use me Lord !!!

Amen

Holy Boldness

Father GOD....Let your grace and glory fill my spirit.

My desire is to be more like you Lord and not like this sinful, prideful and indecisive world.

I can walk in holy boldness and face whatever comes my way today as long as you are with me.

Amen

Spirit of Serenity

GOD grant me the Spirit of Serenity

to accept the things I cannot change.

The courage to change the things I can

and the wisdom to know the difference.

Help me to take one breath, one moment, one day at a time.

Cover me with your love, your peace and your joy.

Knowing that all things are possible if I only believe.

Let me walk in your confidence filled with your Spirit of Serenity.

I will praise your name through times of famine and times of prosperity.

It is in the matchless name of JESUS that I pray knowing that Your will has already been done.

Amen

Transformation
Romans 12

Oh Lord how excellent is thy name in all the earth! Your word says "And be ye not conformed to this world; but, be ye transformed by the renewal of your mind; that ye may prove what is good, and acceptable and the perfect will of God."

Lift us up Lord from the the lowly dusty places where we walk.

Lift us up Lord from the hardened hearts of liars, thieves and fornicators that we call friends.

Lift us up Lord from the desolate places of financial and spiritual lack that we frequent.

Oh Lord how excellent is thy name in all the earth! Transform our minds and carry us to a spiritual place...

Where the air is sweet

Where the sky is blue

Where the grass is green

Where the water is pure

and peace abounds

Renew our spirits Lord and we will continue to give you all of the glory, the honor and the praise.

Amen

My Change

My GOD you are rich in mercy and great with love. I am so glad to know that you love me. You have turned my story around many times. You have brought me out of many trials and tribulations.

I am caught up in the midst of a storm. I am stuck in the middle of a turn around and I seek your guidance. This turn is between only me and you GOD. I am going through my change.

I am a part of the Body of Christ. I come to the Spiritual Mountain for my transformation. I seek to go higher in Christ on this Mount of Transfiguration.

The water has broken. I have cut the cord. I say good-bye to all of the systems, friends and places that held me back. I am moving into a new dimension because a change is coming over my life.

Amen

Prayer Warrior Creed

I WILL SPEAK BOLDLY TO THE UNIVERSE ON HOW MAGNIFICENT AND POWERFUL MY GOD IS YESTERDAY, TODAY AND TOMORROW.

IT DOES NOT MATTER IF I AM GOING INTO A STORM; IN THE MIDST OF A STORM OR COMING OUT OF A STORM FOR I KNOW THAT MY GOD IS WITH ME.

NO MATTER MY STATE OR SEASON; I WILL LIFT MY EYES TO THE HILLS AND I WILL

PRAY

THROUGH

IT

Dr. Deborah D. Dancy
2019

Personal Prayer Practice

On the following pages write 7 personally inspired prayers that the Lord has placed on your heart. You may use the acronym A.C.T.S. as a starting point.

A) Adoration

(C) Confession

(T) Thanksgiving

(S) Supplication

GOD hears all of our prayers from the most simplistic to the most sophisticated. However, this acrostic helps us to organize the different elements of prayer. In addition, it shows us the priority we may want to give to each.

The first element of prayer should be adoration, or praise. We were created to praise GOD. All of our praise, honor and glory belong to Him. He wants us to praise Him.

Second, our prayer should include a confession of our sin. We have all committed some type of sin throughout the day or week; albeit by word, thought or deed. This is the time to talk and turn it over to our Father.

Third, when we pray, we should always give thanks for what the Lord has done, is doing and will do. We thank him for His grace and his mercy for without Him we are nothing.

Fourth, prayer should include supplication or petition for ourselves and others. There is power in the tongue. Use your prayer life as a time to talk to GOD; to meditate on His Word and to Visualize your prayer in action.

I trust that you will find this acrostic helpful for remembering both the elements and the priorities of prayer. Do not be afraid to talk to Our Father. He wants the best for you. You are his masterpiece. Remember, we serve a Living GOD !!!

Faith

A doration

_____

_____

_____

C onfession

_____

_____

_____

T hanks

_____

_____

_____

S upplication

_____

_____

_____

Amen
DDANCY2019

Hope

A doration

_____

_____

_____

C onfession

_____

_____

_____

T hanks

_____

_____

_____

S upplication

_____

_____

_____

Amen
DDANCY2019

Love & Charity

A doration

_____

_____

_____

C onfession

_____

_____

_____

T hanks

_____

_____

_____

S upplication

_____

_____

_____

Amen
DDANCY2019

Courage & Fortitude

A doration

_____

_____

_____

C onfession

_____

_____

_____

T hanks

_____

_____

_____

S upplication

_____

_____

_____

Amen
DDANCY2019

Justice & Equity

A doration

_____

_____

_____

C onfession

_____

_____

_____

T hanks

_____

_____

_____

S upplication

_____

_____

_____

Amen
DDANCY2019

Stewardship & Prudence

A doration

_____

_____

_____

C onfession

_____

_____

_____

T hanks

_____

_____

_____

S upplication

_____

_____

_____

Amen
DDANCY2019

Temperance & Moderation

A doration

_____

_____

_____

C onfession

_____

_____

_____

T hanks

_____

_____

_____

S upplication

_____

_____

_____

Amen
DDANCY2019

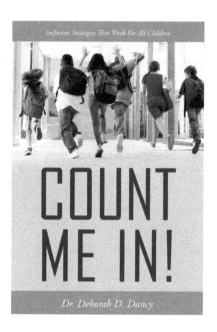

CPSIA information can be obtained
at www.ICGtesting.com
Printed in the USA
FFHW012129101219
56856040-62493FF